Countries for Kids

HELLO

BONJOUR

from

CANADA

C. Manica

Copyright © 2022 by C. Manica

All rights reserved.

No portion of this book may be reproduced in any form without written permission from the publisher or author, except as permitted by U.S. copyright law.

Hello there!
I'm Dustin Beaver.
I'm going to tell you about
my country,
Canada!

So, where is Canada?

Let's look at this map of North America!

This is Canada.

Did you know that Canada and the USA share the longest international border in the world?

Yes, that's right!
It's 8,891 km (5,525 miles) long.

Canada is a very large country, the second largest in the world after Russia!

SECOND PLACE

There are ten provinces and three territories in Canada.

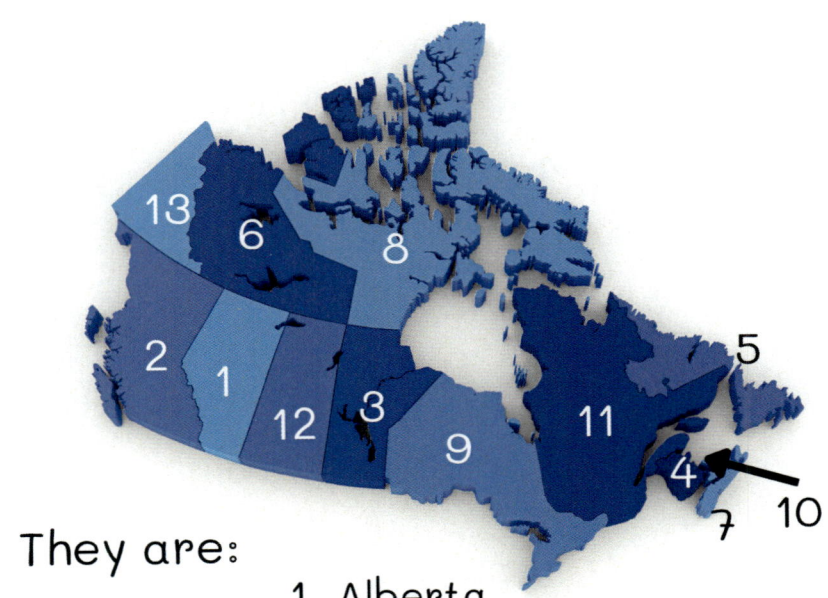

They are:
1. Alberta
2. British Columbia
3. Manitoba
4. New Brunswick
5. Newfoundland and Labrador
6. Northwest Territories
7. Nova Scotia
8. Nunavut
9. Ontario
10. Prince Edward Island
11. Québec
12. Saskatchewan
13. Yukon

Canada is so big, there are six time zones!

From east to west, the time zones are: Atlantic, Eastern, Central, Mountain, and Pacific. Newfoundland has its own time zone.

So, 7 am in Québec is 4 am in British Columbia!

QUÉBEC

BRITISH COLUMBIA

Now, here are some quick facts about Canada!

We have a prime minister, and the head of state is the King of the United Kingdom, who is also the King of Canada.

Our capital is Ottawa. It's in Ontario.

We celebrate our national day, Canada Day, on July 1.

Our currency is the Canadian dollar.

In Canada, a one-dollar coin is called a *loonie*, because it has a picture of a loon (a type of bird) and a two-dollar coin is called a *toonie* because it's worth two loonies.

Canada has not just one but two official languages, English and French. Cool, eh?

It makes sense that our national anthem, "O Canada," has two versions!

Did you know that all products sold in Canada must be labeled in both English and French?

That reminds me, I need to go to the supermarket to buy food!

Let's try some famous Canadian foods!

This is *poutine*. It's French fries with cheese curds and gravy. Yummy!

I love maple syrup on my waffles. Canada is the biggest producer of maple syrup in the world!

In winter, Canadian kids love to eat maple taffy. It's made by pouring boiled maple syrup over snow.

Butter tarts are flaky pastry shells filled with a mixture of butter, sugar, eggs, and syrup. Sometimes raisins, walnuts, or pecans are added to the filling.

Nanaimo bars are a sweet dessert made with a coconut, chocolate, and graham cracker crumb base, a creamy custard middle layer, and a chocolate ganache topping.

Oooh... ketchup and all-dressed chips! I love all-dressed. It's a mix of ketchup, barbecue, salt & vinegar, and sour cream & onion flavors!

Have you tried some Indigenous foods?

This is *bannock*. It's a type of bread that can be baked, pan-fried or deep-fried.

This is *pemmican*. It's a mixture of dried meat and fat. Sometimes berries are added.

You can also find foods from all over the world in Canada....

...because Canada is multicultural. It means there are people from all over the world, from different cultures, living in Canada.

However, the Indigenous people have been living in the area for thousands of years.

The main Indigenous groups in Canada are the Métis, the First Nations, and the Inuit.

Now, let's talk about sports!

We Canadians love hockey...
It's our national sport!

It's a rough sport...
Hockey players have to
wear protective gear
to protect themselves!

You like my new
helmet, eh?
Do you think it's
a bit too big
for me?

With its long winters, Canada is the perfect place to enjoy all kinds of winter sports and activities!

You can try....

skiing,

snowboarding...

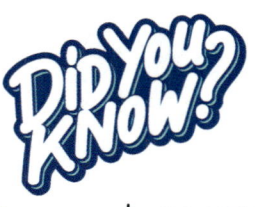

Depending on where you are in Canada, winter can be extremely cold. The coldest temperature ever recorded was -63 °C or -81 °F in Snag, Yukon, in 1947.

13

...tobogganing,

and skating!

Winter in Canada is fun...

...but summer in Canada is fun too!

Summer is generally not too hot in Canada. The temperature ranges between 20 °C (70 °F) to 30 °C (86 °F). However, in some areas, sometimes it can reach 40 °C (104 °F) or even hotter. The hottest temperature ever recorded was 49.6 °C (121 °F) in Lytton, British Columbia, in 2021.

So, what activities can you do in summer?

Well, you can go hiking,

mountain biking,

or camping!

Canada is famous for its beautiful nature!

It's home to hundreds of waterfalls.
The most famous one is Niagara Falls, a huge waterfall located on the Niagara River, in both Canada and the US.

 There are around three million lakes in Canada!

Some of the famous ones are Lake Louise and Moraine Lake in Banff National Park, Alberta, and Maligne Lake in Jasper National Park, also in Alberta.

MORAINE LAKE

LAKE LOUISE

MALIGNE LAKE

17

There are a lot of things you can do at the lake.

You can go...

fishing,

kayaking,

boating,

paddle boarding,

and swimming!

Not all lakes are suitable for swimming, though...

So, don't forget to check what you can and cannot do at each lake, and remember, safety first!

18

Canada has a lot of wildlife.
If you are lucky, you might see some
of these animals...

19

Besides beautiful nature, Canada also has attractive cities.

Toronto, Ontario is the largest city in Canada with so many things to see and do.

You can enjoy the view of Toronto from the CN Tower, explore the Royal Ontario Museum, and try different foods at St. Lawrence Market.

In summer, you can spend the day at Toronto Island Park. There, you can have a picnic, ride a bike, go to the beach, explore Franklin Children's Garden, and see cute animals at the petting farm.

21

Vancouver is a city in British Columbia. It's one of the warmest places in Canada.

There are so many fun things to do in Vancouver!

You can explore Stanley Park, a huge park with a seawall, gardens, playgrounds, and lovely beaches. You can see totem poles (tall carvings by the Indigenous people) there.

Catch a ferry to Granville Island to enjoy a meal at the Public Market, play at the Kids Market, watch live shows, and more!

St. John's, in Newfoundland and Labrador, is a charming city known for its colorful row houses and natural attractions.

You can go to Signal Hill for great views of the city and the sea, and explore the Rooms, a cultural center, museum, and art gallery.

Don't forget to go to Cape Spear Lighthouse for awesome views by the sea!

Calgary is a city in Alberta known for its "cowboy" culture.

Every year, in July, there's a big event called the Calgary Stampede. It's a ten-day celebration with a rodeo, a powwow*, parades, shows, fun rides, foods, and parties!

*First Nations dancing, singing, and drumming competition.

23

Montreal, Québec is the second largest French-speaking city in the world after Paris!

Old Montreal is very beautiful. It's a historic part of the city with cobblestone streets and charming buildings.

At the Old Port of Montreal, you can have lots of fun! Go on a boat ride, play in the parks, visit museums, and more!

You can enjoy amazing views of the city from Mount Royal Park.

Don't forget to visit the Montreal Biosphere! It's a museum and one of Montreal's iconic landmarks.

So now you know a lot about Canada, eh? The food, the people, the sports, the nature, the animals, the cities...

I guess that's all for now....
Bye, *au revoir!*

I ♥ CANADA

Collect all the books in the Countries for Kiddies series!

 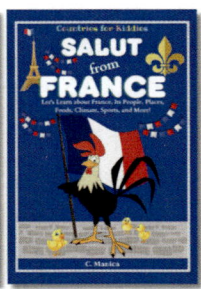  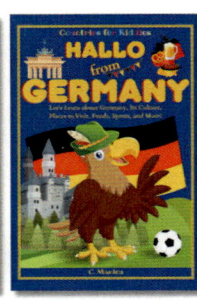 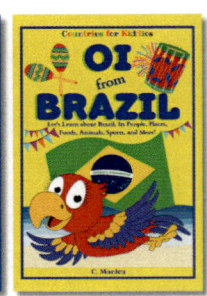

  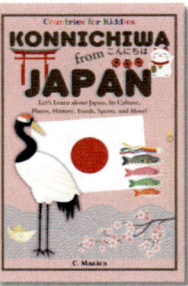  

countries-for-kiddies.com

Made in the USA
Middletown, DE
10 October 2024